To Tovarich Glenn with fond
memories of Leningrad, Kiev,
Moscow, Warsaw and (?) 'East'
Berlin.

EAGregg

REAP SILENCE

REAP SILENCE

E. S. GREGG

McNally and Loftin, Publishers
Charlotte / Santa Barbara

Printed in the United States of America
Heritage Printers, Inc., Charlotte, N. C.

Some of the selections in this volume have previously appeared in *Verses in a Minor Key* (1960), *The New York Evening Post* and *The Statesville Record and Landmark*.

CONTENTS

I

3 Man Sometimes Is Quiet
4 What Shall We Call Man?
5 Affirmation
6 Where I Tread
7 A Query
8 The Searchers
9 Cosmography
10 A Long Thought
11 Origins
12 To A. E. Housman
13 The Poet and You
14 The Enduring
15 Conservation
16 Unreality
17 Tolerance
18 Passage
19 A Revisit

II

23 Epicurean
24 Resignation
25 Payment
26 The Foe

27 Men Hold to Life
28 In Spite of Time
29 Dreams
30 Moods and Time
31 Armor
32 On Growing Older
33 Put Out of Mind
34 Startings
35 A Farewell
36 Innocent Again
37 Estrangement
38 Glamour
39 Duty and I

III

43 Matins
44 Spring
45 Wild Flowers
46 The Indigo Bunting
47 Flower of Neglect
48 A Lament
49 No Black
50 On the Terrace
51 Uninvited
52 Hunger
53 Laughter
54 The Game
55 The Way of a Poet
56 End Piece

I

MAN SOMETIMES IS QUIET

Living is noise among silences.
The wails of birth, the final dirges
are inaudible in the silence of Space
where Earth spins and ears have not
explored. Man's tumults never pierce
the silence of the Ocean's heavy depths
from which simple forms of Life emerged,
as Earth from the sparse dust of Space.
In those darkened, unyielding deeps
survivors hear no moans of the dying
nor shouts of victors. In utter hush
bones undulate and slowly sink
beyond the incipience of breath.
As he unreels his thread of life
Man sometimes is quiet and feels
the patient silences of Sea and Space.
Living is noise among silences.

WHAT SHALL WE CALL MAN?

Shall we call him "homo sapiens,"
This pronged animal, weak in the back,
Who uses at most one sixth of his brain,
Who today toys with the same old vices,
Who faces and combats nothing half
So terrible as himself?

Shall we call him "homo duplex,"
A thing half dust and half divine,
Who had Eden and lost it and who makes Hell
To his specifications and discomfiture,
Who can never justify a vision
Of what he might be and is?

Shall we be forced to call him man
Who has yet to merit an adjective;
Who has salvation in his reach
And also utter devastation,
Who is the despair of himself and his ilk
And the grave concern of God?

What shall we call man?

AFFIRMATION

Through millenia man has sought to solve
What life is and the reasons for it.
It has been said if trivia are husked
Life is only birth and joy and death,
A view which shakes the souls of puritans
Who grieve with guilt if they chance on joy.
And yet briefly I have known ecstasy,
As I stood outside myself and touched
Immortal sensations unknown to nerves.
Who recalls his birth (for memory comes later)
Or a second time has surrendered to Death
So he can say he really knows it?
But joy I know, the joy of living
And I, apart from it, do not exist
Nor ever want to and thus I answer.

WHERE I TREAD

We think the future by chance may differ?
It can only go where the past has been,
Will behold births and ecstasies and deaths
And will wrack the souls of later men.

For where I tread my father trod.
I find no other passage nor stair;
The past, the present, and time to be
Are all up-caught in the changeless air.

This air of buffets and caresses
Brushed Helen's cheeks and will hug the bloom
Of the fissions and fusions of man's perdition
Without a sense of joy or doom.

Tri-part time and circumfusing air:
Faulted dreams and near despair.

A QUERY

All I know begins and ends with I am I,
Disparate, unique by a sacred choice in the reach
Of every man. What tends to hinder me
From being my I am, diminishes me
And is to be resisted. If I do not want
To be I, by choice, then I am not, as if
I ceased to be by drowning in the primal and ultimate
Sea. If compelled to be less than I am by laws
Of congresses or God or by any force whatsoever
Which robs my aloneness, I then cease to be
And also drown in a murky and amorphous mass:
The mediocre. Can it be held wrongful
That I want only to be I and not an average
And thus in my own small way perchance
To cheat the vast forgetfulness of Death?

THE SEARCHERS

From their first askings they are the accursed
Who want truth always with a capital T
And are unconvinced without proofs;
Who doubt, yet insist on accuracy.
They follow their quests without knowing
How much they annoy those who disagree.
There is little happiness in their going.
They search for certainties which may never be
Except in their dreams or for a brief ken.
How lonely they are and yet how free
These thorny, obsessed, and searching men.
For truth sells peace of mind for fees
In harder coin than social niceties.

COSMOGRAPHY

For Dante and Milton the universe was simple.
Heaven was above and Hell was below.
But Science has changed the celestial cosmos
And it differs from what we used to know.

The Earth today is a planet in a galaxy,
Which among others is a very small one.
The Universe itself is expanding outward
And the old religious geography is undone.

We are brought to the truth we have been slow to
accept;
That Heaven and Hell, never far apart,
Can nowhere be located unless within
The prideful, repentant, and glorious Heart.

A LONG THOUGHT

This thought bothers my finite mind:
If everything came from nothingness,
Though destined for final splendor and glory,
What happens, if by miscalculation or error,
Everything ends again in a void?
How can life then be explained or justified,
This life of mine so unutterably sweet,
And why should the mind of man become proud?

ORIGINS

Man often excels, but rarely in obeying;
Hence gallows-rope and altar-fire
Are cudgels to force the most daring
To curb disparity and desire.

The sway of our rulers and our priests
May be the needful and the blessed way;
But when have gibbets and holy fires
Caused thoughts to leap and dreams to play?

TO A. E. HOUSMAN

Your two thin books in thirty years
Take little space on Time's big scales,
And yet, I wager, they outweigh
The works of others sold in bales.

The dreams of youth are heavy stuff,
And thoughts have heft to break young wills,
So lads will drink their ale and boast
Because they would outface their ills.

By gallows and by lead they leave
This world of fitful dreams and breath —
But for your verse they might possess
The oblivion of a common death.

THE POET AND YOU

It is for others to weigh his verses;
   The poet is called on only to sing.
He sings of dreams as vague as sleep
   Or the edge of imagining.
If he opens magical doors for you,
   Uncaring he has done a gladsome thing.
It is for others to weigh his verses;
   The poet is called on only to sing.

THE ENDURING

When things went wry, I have been known
  To sit awhile with Grief,
But now I've met her sister, Sorrow,
  Whose visit will not be brief.

CONSERVATION

As chemicals linked by chance,
Life crept from the primal sea;
Acids and salts and water
Still fashion a house for me,
A house which shall rejoin
The air and changeless sea
And mingle in other forms,
Alike, unlike to me.
And I no longer I
Shall be the sea, the sky.

UNREALITY

A wisp of thought brushed my mind
  Then quickly faded away.
It awoke an echo of a call
  It had made another day.

This confusion of is and was eludes
  The vision of the eye
And leaves a ghostly feeling that
  I am and am not I.

TOLERANCE

On the edge of chaos, the rim of the world,
  Two men stood, one black, one white.
The eternal sun bathed them
  In his immaculate light.

In true clarity the sun saw
  Only two shadows, dark and of a kind,
Cast on the endless desert wastes
  Of the earth and the arrogant mind.

PASSAGE

What fortitude it takes to pass
The lintel of an unknown door,
What courage it takes to cross a street
We have not crossed before!

Bravery in general we seem to know
But not the tiny act of faith
We need to have before we change
Into an ultimate formless wraith.

A REVISIT

Beneath the lintel of the darkening door,
I felt a stirring at our meeting,
Although no answer was returned
To the loud hallo of my greeting.
I sensed a host of memories there,
Wraith-like and ruefully staring
Because I dared a delayed return
From a pilgrimage and distant faring
And had ruined the repose of all of them
Though I was searching for only one.
As I returned from this vain revisit,
I whispered sadly, "You have won."

II

EPICUREAN

> Time at last it is to go, time it is to sleep.
> — Richard le Gallienne,
>   *An Echo from Horace.*

Before you is the world's rich feast,
    Rare peafowl's flesh and mullet roe.
A dullard he who eats the least,
    The lights soon fade, and all must go.

Before you is the strong red wine
    Of love and thought. Up, be not slow!
Drink deep the while the cup is thine,
    The lights soon fade, and all must go.

Before you is the human play,
    More lines of humor than of woe.
Enjoy your laugh, drive frowns away,
    The lights soon fade, and all must go.

And when all things have passed away,
    This verdict Time will then bestow:
They ate and drank and laughed a day,
    The lights went out, they had to go.

RESIGNATION

"This way," I said, "I shall order my days."
  And life made no reply.
But this went wry and that went wrong
  However I would try.

My plans ahead went all askew,
  I faltered on the trail.
In me no king my mother bore
  So how can I prevail?

And I am forced to be content
  To take things as they lie,
For when I argue and fret with life,
  Life has yet to make reply.

PAYMENT

"Take what you wish, but pay," Life said
  When my years totaled a score,
And wishing beyond all possible taking
  I listened to no more.

For I was fired with curiosity
  And lean with hidden hungers
As I tasted the delicacies of
  The grocers, vintners, mongers.

I savored the exhilarations of
  The mind and love and beauty.
But how can I pay for such largess
  Which is my contract duty?

I have not settled my account in full
  Nor do I know a way
And I shall die in debt unless
  I use my breath as pay.

THE FOE

When I look back on my lengthening life,
  Time has been and is the foe
From whom I have wrested learning and love,
  Emotions, colors, and all I know.

For Time is vast and circular,
  Yesterday and all before and tomorrow
And all that is yet to come are caught
  In today's medley of laughter and sorrow.

And in this weary, never-won battle
  Our forebears strained for us as we
Now fight for the future because
  Being mortal we're touched with immortality.

MEN HOLD TO LIFE

Men hold to life by little things,
  By little things, but not for long;
By pride of clan, by creed, conceit —
  Things fragile as a song.

And when they loose their hold on these,
  Life is a worthless thing;
Gone is all beauty from the earth,
  And gone the grace to sing.

IN SPITE OF TIME

Time ravages so many things,
So many things it levels down:
The peasant's crooked staff of thorn,
    The king's great crown.

Proud things and hard it grinds to dust —
So flesh and bone are wont to rot —
But moods, when caught in proper words,
    Are not forgot.

We love? Tomorrow who can say?
Our nerves in other clay may dwell,
And read, perchance, in spite of Time,
    This tale I tell.

DREAMS

Dreams once wrought marvel and surprise
   As many pleasures spiced my days.
They now frustrate my fragile plans
   And rob my peace in endless ways.

Tranquillity is all I wish
   In these my dwindling later years;
And yet what glory was in those dreams
   Of beauty, love, and, yes, of tears!

MOODS AND TIME

Who can measure his moods with Time?
   The mold of equal seconds is a scheme
Of sophists without heft or rhyme.
   Can minutes keep pace with youthful dreams
Or delay our fated audience with Death?
   Ecstasy is always shorter than grief
And Time does not regulate the breath
   Nor make the sense of failure brief.
Living can never be parceled out
   In solar yardsticks of equal years,
But is grasped with clumsiness and doubt
   Between short joys and stinging tears,
Nor can we fetter bit by bit
   In temporal chains, the Infinite.

ARMOR

He said, "Keep armor buckled on;
   It may protect, it cannot save."
He kissed me once, then said goodbye
   And did not turn to wave.

My armor I have duly worn
   About the country and in town.
In daily jousts it wards off blows;
   I dare not lay it down.

I dare not take my armor off,
   I need it now so much to win.
But who makes armor for defense
   When the fight is all within?

ON GROWING OLDER

Comes now this time before decline
When caution chills desire,
When ecstasy is dulled by rote
And restless dreams expire.

Comes this time of pause and calm
With burgeoning relief:
For love exhausts and wit's a strain
And doubt more trying than belief.

This time when thought replaces act
With no room for regret
And no great reason to recall
Or even to forget.

PUT OUT OF MIND

Put out of mind all lovely things:
Forsythia hung with gold in spring.
The plaintive notes of pagan birds,
And every other splendid thing.

With toil we pay for crumbs of bread;
From hostile marts and stony earth
We wrest what nourishment we can,
And helots have no cause for mirth.

Put out of mind all lovely things,
Forget the moonlight on calm waters —
And, most of all, the slender forms
Of Helen's fair, enticing daughters!

STARTINGS

I think my life has started twice:
Once with the dawn of memory
And then again when love first bloomed.
Is there one in immortality?

If I should win this gracious boon,
May it be these two at their high noon.

A FAREWELL

The moon, indifferent and calm,
   Watched us say goodbye.
It did not change its pace
   Across the immaculate sky.

Now high it strides in the heavens
   And sees with mild surprise
That sleep not yet has conquered
   Nor the tears yet dried in my eyes.

INNOCENT AGAIN

Great lauds nor curses on our love
  Could make it by a jot less true;
Else works alone could save the soul
  And evil deed we would not rue.

Beyond man's rules love sanctifies
  A time of marvel and surprise.
It shrives our selfish bents and bids
  Us innocent again to rise.

ESTRANGEMENT

In those young years which vanished in being,
When we found ecstasy more beautiful than the word
So hard to spell, when our hands as of the blind
Saw and our bodies were nearer than near we had
No thoughts of understanding each other, we were
Each other; we were one. The wind never touches the
     same
Cheek twice and a used emotion is forever spent.
The declining sun now casts my shadow over you
And you are unaware of it nor care to whom it belongs.

GLAMOUR

I thought that I was through with love at last.
The pale and haggard face, the wistful eye,
The agonies of doubt were in the past.
The years had given wisdom to defy
The obvious tricks which snare a thoughtless lad.
The joys of love I knew were bought with pain
And some have killed for love and some gone mad —
Who loves can never be himself again.

With pity and a smile I watched the game,
Confident that I could stand apart.
And then — who will may now deride — you came.
My heart, so long indifferent, felt a start,
Incredulous that love, as with a magic wand,
Could bring such glamour when I touched your hand.

DUTY AND I

Duty and I have made our peace
  And I have paid the price,
Because desire is beautiful
  And worth a sacrifice.

Duty and I have made our peace.
  To this I now aspire
That I to you may never be
  Duty without desire.

III

MATINS

As I awoke this morning I heard
The matins the birds were singing
And joy over Rowan, Iredell, and Catawba
Westward with the sun went winging.

SPRING

When Spring, a wanton bright with flowers,
   In city streets is loose,
Such beauty should be caught in words
   For later use.

This exaltation I now feel
   Should never be forgot,
When springs return to Statesville town
   And I do not.

WILD FLOWERS

What beauty is found in the brief wild flowers
   Which appear without tarrying each spring.
Fragile and shy in unplanned array
   They bring a delight past wondering.
They gently proclaim the lack of contest
   Between tame blossoms in their longer faring
And the beauty found in the tiny wild flowers
   Which appear each spring without tarrying.

THE INDIGO BUNTING

The robin in his rufous vest
Is famed as the harbinger of spring.
He whistles several liquid notes
But cannot ever make them sing.

The indigo bunting is small and shy
In his bright coat of turquoise blue.
His song is a melodic tracery
As delicate as webs jeweled with dew.

If the robin would be content to usher
And not try endlessly to sing,
How happy I then would be to hear
The bunting's gentle trouveuring.

FLOWER OF NEGLECT

Where once grew fruit and grain
　By fence and climbing stile,
Now blooms the flower of neglect,
　Wild camomile.

This bitter weed always springs
　And quickly comes to flower
When human ills take hold
　And steal love's power.

Roses, larkspur, mignonette
　In my garden bloomed some while.
Now unattended wildly grows
　Yellow camomile.

A LAMENT

When Summer told me goodbye today,
   The sad-voiced wind in the trees was sighing,
And I am filled with an ageless hurt
   At so much beauty slowly dying.

The zinnias are still a flaming red
   And all the colors are bright and clear,
But the air is chill and endlessly stirring
   As if calamity were somewhere near.

One Summer is passing from my small store
   Beyond even memory or mortal trying,
And I am filled with an ageless hurt
   At so much beauty slowly dying.

NO BLACK

The dogwood berries have turned to red,
The leaves have wearied of being green
One more summer is slowly passing
To limbo's ghostly scene.

As summer now dies it wears no black
But has on colors gay and bright,
All robed and ready in some next world
To greet a greater delight.

ON THE TERRACE

The leaves on the terrace were yellow and red
    And brown and crisp and sere.
The air was chill as it stirred the mists.
    The day was drear.

The wind lunged out and tore the clouds
    That veiled the sun's bright face
And oh! what a dance of colors then
    In that glad place.

UNINVITED

When Pain, the unhoused, the wanderer
    Dropped in on me today,
He wanted to remain a while; I begged
    Him at once to go his way.
Where can he go? He owns no house
    As I to get surcease;
With medicines and drugs we hunt him down
    And relentlessly steal his peace.
Perhaps this once I should decide
    To do a kindly thing
And let him tarry, since, when he's gone,
    I'll have such cause to sing.

HUNGER

Among the legends of ancient Greece
That of King Midas always thrilled
Because, if touch turned all to gold,
Greed at last could be killed.

But even the Greeks were not allwise
And after many years I wonder
If by far the richest gift of the gods
Has not been and is not hunger.

LAUGHTER

As to a metronome the years
Dance in steps measured and severe.
They often elicit japes and smiles
But lack the heft to engender fear.

We have one chance — we shall get no more —
To prove why we have use of Earth.
The ears of Time never give heed
To grave-side griefs nor cries at birth.

We breathe, love briefly, too soon are gone.
As we curvet or shuffle to the tunes Time plays
The only riposte within our scope
Is to laugh throughout the vacuous days.

THE GAME

Death and I played vignt-et-un in jest —
His list was slack that day and lacked my name —
We talked of now and after, but when I said,
"Your denial of pleas for the shortest reprieves
And your perverse pride condemn you as a tyrant;
Science should exile you from Earth," the light
Grew dim and anger flared from his hollow eyes.
"A card?" he asked. My dilemma was fifteen; I stood.
He chanced another, then shrugged, "You win this time,
But Science lacks pith to banish me from Man."
As he vanished, he said, "I lay claim to one more game."